Marquetry

The How-to-do-it Book
by Jack Garside

The Vestal Press, Ltd.
Vestal, New York

Other Vestal Press books in woodcarving

Carving Your Own Carousel Animal by Gene Bass

Carving Weathered Wood: Tips and techniques for award-winning carvings by Gene Bass and Jack Portice

Carving Miniature Carousel Animals: Country Fair Style
   by Jerry Reinhardt

and distributed through Vestal Press:
Whittling Simplified by Herb Reinecke (AlMar Press)

The Vestal Press, Ltd., PO Box 97, Vestal, New York 13850

Printed in the United States of America
99 98 97 96   9 8 7 6 5 4 3 2 1

Library of Congress Cataloging-in-Publication Data

Garside, Jack, 1915-
      Marquetry: the how-to-do-it book / by Jack Garside
            p. cm.
      ISBN 1-879511-01-0 (PBK: A-Free)
      1. Marquetry. I. Title
      TT192.g37 1992
      745.51--dc20   92-13174
                                                  CIP

• Contents •

To Harold and Ron

• Introduction •

Marquetry is an ancient craft in which thin wood veneers with a variety of grains and colors are glued onto a flat, wooden surface to make pictures or decorative patterns for furniture, jewelry boxes, etc. *Parquetry* is the same idea but uses a geometric pattern. *Inlay* differs from both of these two crafts in that some of the backing is routed out and veneer is inserted into the routed portions.

Some examples of parquetry have been found that date back to 3000 B.C., and objects using parquetry were found in the tomb of Tutankhamen. The Egyptians' method of cutting is not known, but the designs were geometric patterns of herringbone and basketweave.

During the Dark Ages, monasteries in northern Italy developed mosaic patterns for their church furniture that used wood colors and grains as their primary focus.

In the Gothic times of the 12th to 15th centuries, the shoulder knife (so-called because the handle was long enough to rest on the shoulder while the blade was manipulated) was invented to cut veneers. Resting the handle on the shoulder eliminated the pivoting action of the hand that results when cutting through a piece of veneer with a small blade. The craftsman could use the leverage of his own body to maneuver the knife so that he could concentrate on following the cutting line. This is a distinct advantage if thick or hardwood veneers are cut; until modern times, the craftsman made his own veneers, which could be up to ¼" thick. Simple designs with curves — flowers, leaves, tendrils, etc. — could now be made using a shoulder knife, an advancement to inlaid marquetry designs from former inlaid parquetry designs. Examples of this kind of work can still be seen in museums and churches throughout Europe. Modern-day availability of precision-sliced, thin veneers and improved cutting methods have eliminated the need for shoulder knives.

Furniture styles have determined what marquetry patterns were in vogue at any given time throughout history. It has only been in relatively recent times that marquetry has been used in a picture form, rather than as decoration for furniture. Examples of cabinets from the Italian Renaissance show the high art form to which marquetry rose during this era. These furniture creations were and are greatly admired — incredible legacies of the skills of the men belonging to the marquetry guilds.

During the 15th and 16th centuries, Fra Damiano da Bergamo, a Dominican friar, was considered the finest artist in woods. In his later work, he used dyes and chemically treated woods to give marquetry a painting style. His work survives in museums in Bologna.

However, marquetry is most successful when it does not imitate brushwork painting but stands on its own merits. Materials for each type of work are different — as are techniques. When marquetry artists began to use brush strokes to "enhance" their work, marquetry as an art form declined.

The invention of the fret saw in 1562 revived interest in this skill and enabled craftsmen to assemble the veneers in an overlay, rather than inlay, form. At about the same time, a veneer mill in Germany developed the ability to cut veneers much thinner — about ⅛". This revived the practice of marquetry considerably. Furniture function became secondary to lavish designs covering every possible surface of the wood, and the shape of the design became more important than the types of woods used in the design.

Marquetry reached another high in virtuosity and technique under the patronage of King Louis XIV, the Sun King of France. Masters of marquetry from this age include Andre Charles Boulle, Charles Cresscent, and Jean Henri Riesener.

However, David Roentgen, who worked near Koblenz, Germany, was the outstanding marquetry master of the day. He produced spectacular cabinets and wall panels for royal palaces in Berlin and St. Petersburg, Russia. His scenes from classical mythology used tiny pieces of white and dark woods to produce such subtle shadings that the completed work resembled a pen-and-ink etching. Marie Antoinette summoned Roentgen to her court in 1774.

But by the beginning of the 19th century, interest in this art form had peaked and was dying out again. Furniture became functional and, later, carved ornamentation became more important. In the 20th century, mass-produced furniture and a demand for sleek, uniform, and box-like styles caused marquetry to be all but forgotten.

Today, however, we see a renewed interest in antique crafts, and many people now have the leisure time to pursue these activities. Most projects today are of the picture variety, but using marquetry to decorate furniture, cabinet doors, small boxes, and chess and backgammon boards is increasingly intriguing to craftsmen. Unlike other woodworking hobbies, it does not require expensive tools, materials, or brawn. It is a satisfying way to create something original of great and lasting beauty.

1 • Tools and Supplies

Tools are a critical part of any craftsman's project. There is nothing so annoying as a knife that will not hold an edge or a square that is slightly off 90 degrees. Buy the best tools that you can afford. Poor tools reduce the pleasure of any endeavor. The following list represents the tools that I use; any equivalent tools would be satisfactory.

Woodworking Tools and Supplies

1. *Straightedge*, 24 inches long and made of metal because it will be used to guide a knife blade

2. *Combination square* with 12-inch blade

3. *Magnifying visor*

4. *Scalpel handle and blades*, No. 11. A warning about the danger inherent in scalpel blades: THEY ARE SHARP AND CUT VERY EASILY. Even with this hazard, they are safer than a dull blade. The sterilized handle and blades are available at surgical supply houses and some drug stores.

5. *Whetstone and oil*

6. Sharp, pointed *tweezers*, 4 or 5 inches long

7. *Scroll saw*. I have a saw with a 4-speed belt drive. A better choice would have been a machine with a variable-speed control.

   In selecting a saw, remember that the throat dimension governs the size of wood or other material that the machine will cut. A small machine with a 14-inch throat is

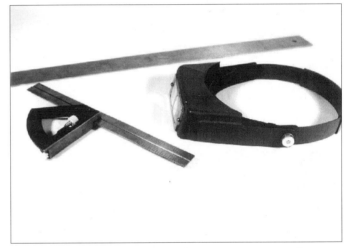

Fig, 1-1. A straightedge, a combination square, and a magnifying visor.

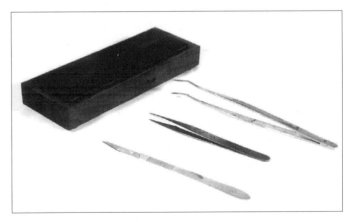

Fig. 1-2. Scalpel handle and blades, a whetstone, and tweezers.

adequate for almost any marquetry project. An important consideration for any machine is the method of securing the saw blade and the ability to slow the cutting speed. Perhaps some of the less expensive machines would suffice, but pay careful attention to these two problems. It may be possible to add a

3

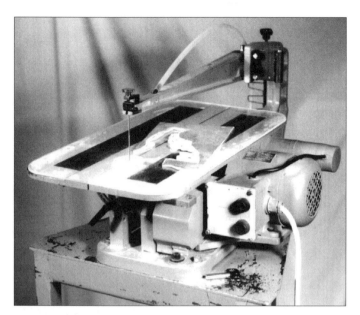

Fig. 1-3. Coping saw.

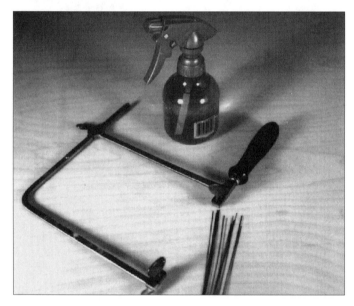

Fig. 1-4. Fret saw, jewelers saw blades, and a water spray bottle.

Fig. 1-5. A swatch of veneer and *Fine Hardwoods Selectorama* book.

Fig. 1-6. Toothed glue-spreading trowel, sanding blocks, and sandpaper.

commercially available electronic speed control, but an inquiry should be made to determine whether the control and motor are compatible. A mismatch could result in the destruction of the motor.

Quick and easy replacement of saw blades is an important consideration in choosing any saw. Coping saw blades have a transverse pin at each end of the blade to secure it to the saw frame. Jeweler's blades, on the other hand, are too small to accommodate pins and are clamped into the machine.

All blade guards or hold-downs that obstruct the view of the cutting line need to be removed. At the end of this chapter is an explanation and drawing of an auxiliary table top that is secured to the machine table; it is needed to cut veneers successfully.

8. *Fret saw frame.*

9. *Jewelers saw blades*, No. 4x0. I buy them by the gross (for about $25) as I break about fifty per project. I use either Swiss or German manufactured blades. I know of no domestic blade that will outlast them. They can be obtained from specialty hardware stores. A jewelry repair shop will not have the quantity

you need, but they will sometimes order them for you.

10. *Hand stapler*

11. *Veneers* are readily available but usually not locally. The best way to locate the many sources is to obtain one of the craftsman magazines.

When ordering veneers, remember that in most cases, the 800 telephone number is for credit card orders only, but a catalogue will usually be sent if the operator is specifically asked for one.

Most vendors offer a set of about fifty samples in a box for a nominal cost. These samples, along with the book *Fine Hardwoods Selectorama*, will assist a craftsman in choosing a particular wood for a certain effect. This book can be ordered from

FINE HARDWOODS/AMERICAN
WALNUT ASSOCIATION
5603 West Raymond St. Suite O
Indianapolis, IN 46241

12. *White, clean sand*

13. *Illustration or poster board*

14. *Aliphatic resin glue.* There are veneer contact cements on the market, one of which I used on a large 24" x 36" picture — to my sorrow. After about five years, the butts, burls, and crotches of the veneers started to lift off the core piece of plywood; in another year, the rest of the picture started to go. The damage was so extensive that the picture was not repairable. Contact cement is a lot easier to use, but its durability is questionable, so I recommend the aliphatic resin glue.

15. *Toothed glue-spreading trowel*

16. *Rubber cement and thinner*

17. *Newspapers*

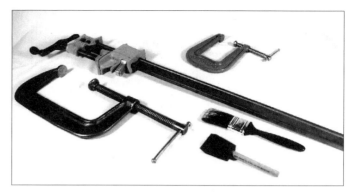

Fig. 1-7. Paint brushes, "C clamps" and "I" bar clamps.

18. *Waxed paper*

19. *Veneer press*

20. *Rubber sanding blocks*; ideally, one for each grade of sandpaper that will be used.

21. *Sandpaper*, open-coat garnet or (better yet) silicon-carbide paper. Open-coat is preferable; closed-coat will cut faster, but has a tendency to clog. Sanding seldom requires a grade rougher than 120-grit. I use a 200-grit for the intermediate stage, and 400-grit wet or dry for the final.

22. *Spray bottle* for water

23. *Polyurethane clear-gloss finish.* It is important to use a varnish that preserves the original colors of the veneers. This finish will fill that need although there seems to be an amber cast to the contents of the opened can.

24. *Disposable foam paint brushes*

25. *"C" clamps*

26. Two steel *"I" bar clamps* with 24-inch openings

27. *Automotive polishing compound*, optional

The Veneer Press

For pictures less than 10" x 12", an antique book press makes an excellent veneer clamp for gluing the assembled veneer picture and the

Fig. 1-8. An antique book press.

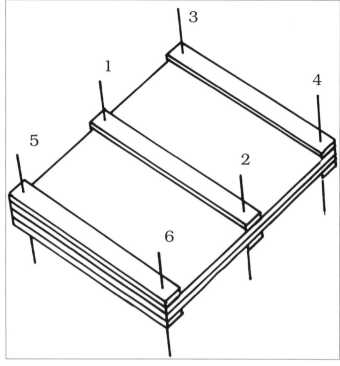

Fig. 1-10. Clamping sequence.

backing to the core. It does have a few disadvantages. Simultaneous pressure is applied all over the panel, which may trap air or excess glue within the picture area. Also, if the screw is over-tightened, too much pressure can be applied to the veneer, breaking down the adhesive quali-

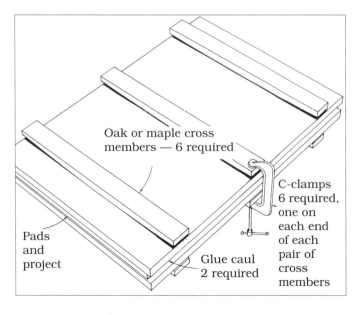

Oak or maple cross members — 6 required

C-clamps 6 required, one on each end of each pair of cross members

Pads and project

Glue caul 2 required

Fig. 1-9. A simple veneer press.

ties of the glue, and/or damaging the veneer. I have never had any problem with mine, but if any of these things were to happen, the entire project would have to be started again.

A simple veneer press is easy to make according to the following instructions. As shown in figure 1-9, it requires two pieces of good grade, perfectly flat, ¾-inch plywood to back up the veneer. These pieces are known as cauls. They accept the pressure of the clamps and cross pieces, and distribute it evenly over the surface of the veneer. The length and width of the cauls must be larger than the project being glued. The cross pieces must be of hardwood — either oak or maple. Make enough of them so that there is one pair for each six inches of caul length. They should be 2 inches wide and 1½" thick; the length is the same as the width of the cauls. The cross members should have a gradual arc in the area that contacts the caul; this arc should have a rise of about ³⁄₁₆ inches between center and ends. This ensures that when pressure is applied, it will originate in the center and, as the clamps are tightened, excess glue or air pockets will be forced out to the edges. The clamps continue to be tightened until the bowed surface of each cross member is straight, and pressure is

Fig. 1-11. A veneer press.

If it seems that excessive tightening of the clamps is required to apply pressure to the edge of the picture, thin down the cross members.

A more versatile press is required by anyone who is going to put a lot of time and effort into marquetry. The following specifications and drawing discuss such a press:

1. Nine 9-inch Pony "Little Giant" *press screws*

2. Six 2" x 4" x 21" *pieces of oak or maple*

3. Twelve 1" x 2" x 12" *pieces of oak or maple*

4. Twelve 1" x 2" x 2" *pieces of oak or maple*

5. Two 18" x 20" pieces of cabinet-grade, ¾-inch *plywood*

applied out to the perimeter of the pictures. Tightening the clamps should be done in sequence as illustrated in Figure 1-10.

When using this press, remember to tighten the press screws in the center first and gradually work out to the perimeter.

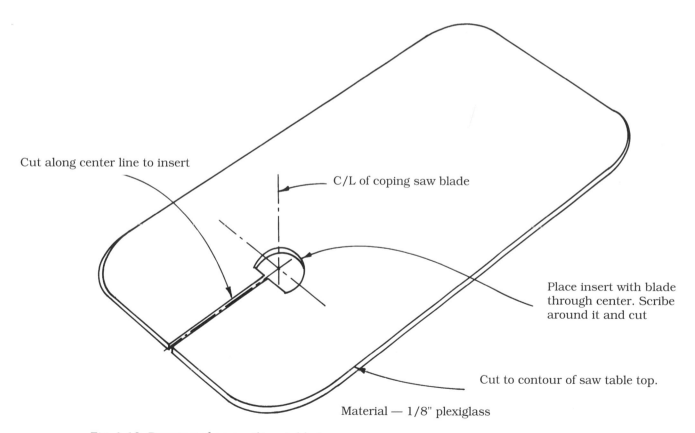

Cut along center line to insert

C/L of coping saw blade

Place insert with blade through center. Scribe around it and cut

Cut to contour of saw table top.

Material — 1/8" plexiglass

Fig. 1-12. Drawing of an auxiliary table top.

Auxiliary Table Top for Coping Saw

The table tops of all saws have large apertures for the saw blade. The hole will accommodate blades of various sizes for other jobs for which the machine can be used. It is wise to keep in mind that when the saw is being used for cutting any material, the blade will roam quite a bit in the aperture and break if it contacts the steel table top. When cutting wood for marquetry, it is necessary to reduce the size of the opening so that there is some support underneath the veneer as it is being cut. A smaller opening will also prevent small pieces of the veneer from going right through the table top along with the saw blade.

One way to have a smaller opening is to make an auxiliary table top of ⅛" Plexiglas™ or an equivalent plastic. Keep in mind that the saw blade should have a light tension when operating in order to lessen saw breakage, and that the blade will wander from side to side when cutting any material. This wandering enlarges the blade slot and means replacing the subsidiary table top when the slot becomes too large. Another (and cheaper) way to have a smaller opening is to use just an insert in the area where the saw blade goes through the secondary table top. It is obviously more sensible to replace a portion of the top rather than the whole thing. A quantity of ⅛" plexiglass inserts needs to be on hand for this method of making the opening small enough to work with tiny pieces of veneer.

If a drill press is not available, and the procedures of woodworking are not familiar, it may be advantageous to have someone make the supplementary table-top inserts. They are

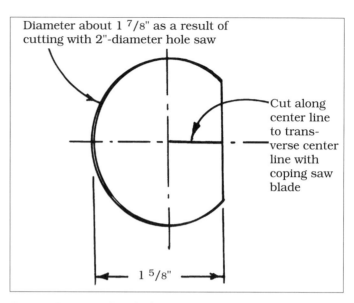

Fig. 1-13. Insert detail of auxiliary table top.

made with a 2" hole saw that has the pilot drill removed. The hole saw must be chucked in a drill-press to compensate for the lack of guidance that the pilot drill would otherwise provide. For the sake of safety, secure the plastic to the drill press table with a "C" clamp. A piece of plywood between the Plexiglas™ and the steel of the drill press table will prolong the life of the saw.

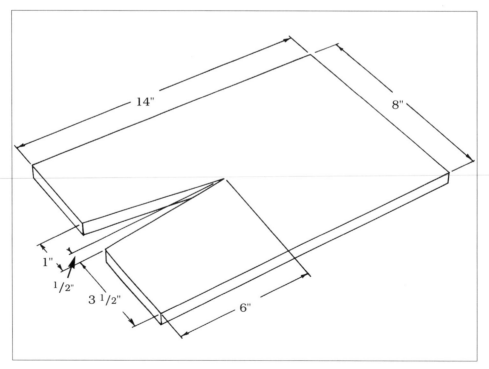

Fig. 1-14. Birdsmouth.

The best way to cut the hole for the insert in the subsidiary table top is to use an insert as a guide, tracing around this insert with a stylus. Cut the opening close to the inside of the stylus line, remembering that it is better to have to enlarge the hole with a file than to reduce it.

An alternative to a somewhat expensive coping saw is a fret saw cutting table (commonly called a Birdsmouth), a "C" clamp, and a fret-saw. These items are available from vendors that specialize in marquetry supplies. Illustration 1-14 of the birdsmouth can serve as a guide for constructing one if it is made at home; all dimensions are approximate.

To use the Birdsmouth properly, it must be clamped to a table top. Fret saws are available with various throat sizes; the size chosen will depend on the largest piece of veneer needing to be cut. The saws with the lesser throat depth are easier to use, so it may be advisable to buy two saws — one with a 3" and the other with an 8" throat. Almost all cutting can be handled with the smaller saw.

The actual cutting with a Birdsmouth is performed in the same way that the power saw would do it: one hand provides the up and down motion to the fret saw, and the other hand guides the veneer pad. The blade should be as perpendicular as possible, and the cutting line must be followed so that there are no wide gaps when the veneer pieces are fitted together.

2 • Creating a Pattern

Most marquetry kits that can be bought today have machine-cut pieces. These kits have veneer parts that are assembled like a jigsaw puzzle, glued to a piece of plywood that is also a part of the kit, sanded, and then finished. These kits do not include a veneer press for adhering the veneers to the plywood core or the necessary finishing materials to complete the job, but they are an excellent way to get acquainted with this fascinating hobby. There are a few kits on the market that are not pre-cut and include the various veneers, patterns, and glue for the project. The kit veneers need to be cut as the patterns indicate and then glued to a plywood core just as pre-cut veneers are. The advantage of buying a kit is that a large stock of veneers does not have to be on hand. Again, however, a press and finishing materials are not included in these kits.

Getting Started in Marquetry

A membership in THE MARQUETRY SOCIETY OF AMERICA is a good way to get involved in this hobby. The address for this organization is:
P. O. Box 224
Lindenhurst NY 11757

A postcard to that address will provide an application, information on cost, etc. One of their many advantages is a monthly newsletter with several featured patterns. They also have an extensive library of designs at all levels of complexity. These designs are accessible to members at a nominal cost. Another benefit is a list of other members and their addresses, which enables a member to contact another member who lives close by and who might share an interest in this hobby.

The first example of marquetry that I saw was created by a local carpenter. I decided to give it a try, and I have been doing it ever since. I bought a craftsman's magazine and sent for catalogues from every veneer house in the periodical. I ordered sample packages from one of the vendors and a few combination veneer specials from others. One dealer offered 25 pounds of loose ends for a very low cost. I think they swept up the warehouse and sent me every loose end in the place — certainly more than 25 pounds. There were no excessively large pieces, but they were perfect for what I wanted.

Tools and Supplies for Making Patterns

1. *Drawing pen* with 4 x 0 (.18) nib

2. *Pencils, erasers*, etc.

3. *India ink*

4. *Picture* with bold, simple outlines

5. *Tracing vellum*

6. *Talcum powder*

7. *Masking tape*

Choosing Veneer or Subject First

There are two ways to begin a project. One way is to choose a veneer with grain and characteristics that seem to convey a mood, and then locate or draw a picture with its largest area representing that mood. The other way is to

Fig. 2-1. Parquetry.

needing to be shaded or have the tone changed slightly, choose a veneer leaf that is naturally discolored. Chapter Three discusses how to shade the wood artificially with heated sand and introduces woods that are colored by chemical processes and dyes.

For a first attempt, select a simple picture or pattern with few components. It is easy to become discouraged if the project seems to drag out, so a first endeavor should be one that can be completed in a reasonable length of time. Fortunately, this craft has various levels of complexity, and there is a sense of accomplishment when each of the various stages is mastered. An easy first attempt might be a geometric pattern; this type of woodworking is known as parquetry. In this version of the hobby, almost all of the cutting is done with a knife and, in some cases, parts are duplicated many times over.

Enlarging the Line Drawing

The first few steps consist of converting the picture to a line drawing, which is then reproduced on a copying machine. Then all of the veneers are cut from patterns on the copies and rubber cemented to a reversed copy. Treat each one of these phases as a triumph.

The following photos show the stages in creating a pattern. The original picture is a photograph taken in Burano which is one of the islands in the Venice Lagoon, Italy. The photograph (Figure 2.2) measures 3½ x 5 and was enlarged 300 percent by a local copying service,

select a picture and then find veneer that represents the largest area.

Some examples of marquetry depend only on differences in wood color to create a design. I prefer to rely on the inherent grain and color of the wood for the effect that I want. Remember to start with the area that will require the largest piece of veneer. It could suggest a storm — either in the sky or a rough sea. Perhaps it reminds the craftsman of the desert. Use that veneer around which to build a picture.

If a picture has already been picked out for the project, look at the veneer inventory and choose one for the largest area of picture that imparts the feeling of that area. This search for mood cannot be applied to all the parts of the picture. Some pieces are too small to show any grain or character. In such cases, the veneer should simply provide a contrast to the pieces next to it.

Excellent projects can be derived from pictures in magazines, postcards, or photographs. The craftsman who is also skilled in drawing or sketching should get a sketch pad and go all the way, making the design original as well as the veneer choices. Regardless of how the picture is chosen, it should have clearly defined borders for each type of wood to fit. If there is an area

Fig. 2-2. A photograph and line drawing of Burano.

Fig. 2-3. Extended lines on a line drawing.

expanding the picture to 10½ x 15 and a line drawing was traced from it. A pantograph can be used to increase the size of a picture, but using an enlarging copier is much easier and less time-consuming.

Transferring the Drawing to Vellum

After the picture has been enlarged to the desired size, cover it with a sheet of inking vellum and secure it to a drawing board with masking tape before beginning to ink in the lines. Vellum has a tendency to pick up oils from a person's hands, and india ink will not adhere to these oily spots. This situation causes holidays or incomplete lines. Before doing any inking, it is best to remove this residue by sprinkling some talcum powder on the vellum, spreading it around with a

Fig. 2-4. The dingy in "Tidal Basin".

cloth and wiping it off. Try to avoid touching the vellum with the fingers, but if broken lines begin to appear later in the inking process, repeat the powder treatment.

Later on, when it is time to fit the borders to the picture, about ¼ of an inch of the wood will need to be trimmed from each edge of the picture to even up all of the sides. Compensate for this step right now in the inking process by extending the lines of each section on the edge of the picture by ¼", as shown in Figure 2-3.

All lines on the drawing will have to meet another line wherever different veneers will come together. Otherwise, during the cutting operation, the coping-saw operator will come to a dead end with no idea of where to go next. It is a good idea to go over the finished drawing and check each line to make sure that it forms an enclosure. However, there are exceptions. Occasionally lines are needed for an effect and not separation of veneers; there will be the same kind of wood on both sides of the line. It will make it easier if an arrow to indicate the grain direction is drawn on each piece of the design that will be cut separately from veneers.

Choosing Veneers

As mentioned previously, the ideal design originates from the natural grain or features of a sheet (commonly called a leaf) of veneer. The figures or imperfections might suggest a picture, and the complete design evolves from that cue. I have seen an award-winning picture that was made almost completely from a single leaf of veneer. The grain and color of the wood gave an impression of a realistic sea, horizon, and sky. The only other veneer piece used in that picture was a dark silhouette of a boat that was inserted in an appropriate place in the picture. The result was very effective. To be able to do this, it is necessary to be very familiar with the veneers on hand. Often, it is possible to use the grain or imperfections in the wood to provide a detail. The inside view of the dinghy planking in the foreground of Tidal Basin was created by picking a veneer leaf with a suitable grain.

This choice eliminated cutting and gluing many pieces of different kinds of veneers.

A log from a tree consists of sapwood and heartwood. The sapwood contains living cells and is the active part of the life process of the tree. Heartwood, on the other hand, consists of inactive cells formed by changes in the inner cells of the sapwood. The sapwood could extend from ½" in depth to 6 inches, depending on the type of tree and environmental factors. Usually the color and grain of the two woods are different so that if the veneer has been plain-sliced or quarter-sliced, both types will appear on each leaf of veneer.

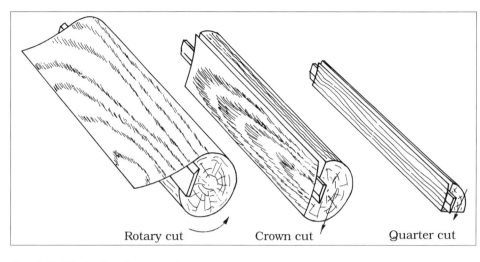

Rotary cut   Crown cut   Quarter cut

Fig. 2-5. Methods of veneer slicing.

If the veneer has been rotary or half-round cut, the veneer will be either sapwood or heartwood, but not both.

A picture of a gull perched on a piling looked like a project that might fit a piece of veneer that I had in stock. The grain in the heartwood indicated disturbed water, the demarcation line between heartwood and sapwood formed the horizon, and the sapwood suggested a realistic sky. This piece saved a great deal of cutting and made a pleasing picture.

Copying the Drawing

After completing the inking process, make enough copies of the vellum drawing so that each section can be cut out from a sheet separately without interfering with any other area. When a section is cut out for a certain veneer, the sections around it will have be cut into; a complete pattern of many parts cannot be made with one copy. I normally make twelve copies.

When making copies, place a clean, white sheet of paper in back of the tracing vellum to provide clearly defined lines for the cutting operation.

A reversed-image copy will also be needed. For this copy, just turn over the vellum drawing in the copier and back it up with the sheet of white paper. If more than one marquetry project of one picture will be done at one time, a mirror-

Fig. 2-6. "Gull" picture.

Fig. 2-7. Reversed image copy.

reversed copy will be needed for each project, i.e., if veneers for six identical pictures will be cut out at the same time, six reversed reproductions will be needed. The pieces of veneer are assembled and rubber cemented to their place on this reversed copy. When it is time to glue the veneer to its plywood core, the veneer side will simply be laid on the glue that has been spread on the plywood core.

All copying must be done on the same machine and in the same time frame. The modern copier utilizes an optical system, and the output from one machine is not exactly the same as that produced on another. If parts of a picture are cut from copies made on two different copiers, the resulting veneer components may not fit together properly. The lines on the pattern are critical and must be identical from copy to copy.

3 • Choosing Veneers

The most important part of a successful marquetry project is choosing the veneers. Wood has color but rarely will it match the actual shade of the sky, trees, sea, etc. Instead, the grain, or pattern, of the wood has to convey that impression. The first thing to do is to choose a veneer for the largest area of the picture. If it is the sky, look for grain lines in the wood or a general appearance that seems to convey that impression. If the largest part of the picture is the sea, then the grain lines could suggest water that is still and smooth, or rough and wind-swept. If the picture has areas meant to convey sunshine, then light colors are needed. If a somber picture is desired, the colors chosen should be dark.

Most veneers have a varied spacing between grain stripes. These stripes are the growth rings of the tree; because the tree grows faster at an early age, the rings are spaced further apart near the center of a log. This phenomenon is to the craftsman's advantage. In choosing wood for the sky or the sea, position the veneer so that the rings spaced closest together will be near the horizon of the picture — further away from the eye in the final picture. This helps to convey a sense of depth perspective.

Another way to give the perception of depth to a scene is to take advantage of the differences in shading of the wood. Align the design and veneer so that the darkest area of the wood will be in the distance of the picture.

The veneer can also be lightly charred and darkened artificially with hot sand to achieve this effect. The piccc is dipped into the sand with tweezers, or the sand can be ladled with a spoon onto the area that needs to be darkened. A warning about heating sand: IT GETS EXTREMELY HOT, so do not get any on fingers or hands. Use an iron skillet or pan to heat the sand because an aluminum pan will burn through and make a real mess of the kitchen stove (author's experience). Sand shading is very useful when two of the same kinds of woods come together. As an example, a ship's sails may all be of the same kind of wood, but the impression of one being behind another is needed. To delineate between the two, shade the mating edge of one of them, and there will be two sails instead of a white blob.

The following list of veneers helps in choosing the kinds of wood that could be used in marquetry or parquetry projects. These veneers were all available at the time this book was written, but the market fluctuates; all too often, some woods fall into the "rare" category. Supplemental information is contained in the previously mentioned book *Fine Hardwoods Selectorama*. The beauty of these woods cannot be conveyed in a list such as this one, so I strongly recommend the purchase of this publication with its color photographs and complete descriptions of hues and patterns.

AMARANTH, BOIS VIOLET, MORADO, NAZARENO, PURPLEHEART, or VIOLETWOOD
    Source: Dutch Guiana
    Color: Purple
    Pattern: Mild stripe and mottled grain

ASH, JAPANESE or TAMO
    Source: Japan
    Color: Brown to tan through gray to almost white
    Pattern: Plain to highly varied with swirls; fiddleback mottle and "peanut shell" figure

15

ASH, OLIVE
- Source: England, France, Turkey, and Hungary
- Color: White and brown
- Pattern: Burl

ASH, WHITE
- Source: United States
- Color: Cream to light brown
- Pattern: Straight, moderately open grain

ASPEN or POPLAR
- Source: United States
- Color: Pure white to light yellow
- Pattern: Mostly crotches and swirls

AVODIRE or APAYA
- Source: Africa
- Color: White to creamy gold
- Pattern: Largely figured with a mottle, crotches, and swirls

BEECH
- Source: United States and Europe
- Color: Red-brown
- Pattern: Straight grain

BENGE, AMAZAQUE, MOZAMBIQUE, OVENKOL, KOLIMA, ANOKHE, or HYEDUANINI
- Source: Africa
- Color: Golden-brown
- Pattern: Plain and contrasting; some figures

BENIN, TIGERWOOD, or CONGO WOOD
- Source: Africa
- Color: Grey-brown to gold with black streaks
- Pattern: Pronounced ribbon stripes

BIRCH, WHITE
- Source: United States and Canada
- White: Cream or light brown tinged with red
- Pattern: Plain, often curly or wavy grain

BUBINGA, AFRICAN ROSEWOOD, AKUME, or KEVAZINGO
- Source: Africa
- Color: Red with streaks of dark purple
- Pattern: Stripe and heavy grain

BUTTERNUT or WHITE WALNUT
- Source: United States
- Color: Warm buttery tan
- Pattern: Satiny with leafy grain

CEDAR, AROMATIC RED or JUNIPER
- Source: United States
- Color: Light red, streaks of light
- Pattern: Knotty

CHERRY, BAKU, CHERRY MAHOGANY, or MAKORE
- Source: Africa
- Color: Pink-brown to blood red or red brown
- Pattern: Some straight grain and some figures. Somewhat similar to a fine grain Mahogany.

CHERRY, AMERICAN BLACK
- Source: United States
- Color: Light red-brown
- Pattern: Straight-grained, satiny, some figures

EBONY, GABOON, BLACK, CAMEROON, or NIGERIAN or CALABAR
- Source: Africa
- Color: Very deep black
- Pattern: Indistinct grain

EBONY, MACASSAR
- Source: India
- Color: Dark brown to black
- Pattern: Brown streaks on black

ELM, AMERICAN. Also GRAY, WHITE, SOFT, or WATER
- Source: United States
- Color: Light gray-brown to pinkish-brown
- Pattern: Straight to sometimes interlocked grain

ELM, CARPATHIAN or ENGLISH
- Source: England and France
- Color: Brick-red to light tan
- Pattern: Medium to fine burl

16

EUCALYPTUS
  Source: Australia
  Colors and Patterns: Wide range

GONCALO ALVES, KINGWOOD, GATEADO, or MURA
  Source: Brazil
  Color: Dark brown
  Pattern: Dark brown with black bands and brown streaks

GUMWOOD, RED, SOUTHERN, or SWEET
  Source: United States
  Color   Red-brown
  Pattern: Dark streaks, often figured

HAREWOOD, ENGLISH SYCAMORE, PLANE, or GREAT MAPLE
  Source: England
  Color: Natural white, usually dyed silver gray
  Pattern: Plain and figured

HICKORY
  Source: United States
  Color: White to cream
  Pattern: Fine brown lines

HOLLY
  Source: United States
  Color: Very white
  Pattern: Close-grained; almost no visible pattern

IMBUYA, BRAZILIAN WALNUT, DETERMA, EMBUIA, or IMBUIA
  Source: Brazil
  Color: Rich brown
  Pattern: Usually burls

KELOBRA, GUANACASTE, GENICERO, JENISERO, or PAROTA
  Source: Mexico
  Color: Brown with green cast
  Pattern: Large figure with wavy lines

KOA
  Source: Hawaii
  Color: Golden brown
  Pattern: Dark brown streaks, lustrous sheen

LACEWOOD or SILKY OAK
  Source: Australia
  Color: Light pink with silver sheen
  Pattern: Small flaky grain

LIMBA, LIMBO, AFARA, FRAKE, or OFFRAM
  Source: Africa
  Color: Pale yellow to light brown
  Pattern: Grain is fine and irregular

MADRONE
  Source: United States
  Color: Red-brown
  Pattern: Close-grain burl

MAHOGANY, AFRICAN
  Source: Africa
  Color: Light pink to red-brown and tan-brown
  Pattern: Plain stripe, broken stripes, mottle, fiddleback, fine crotches, and faux swirl

MAHOGANY, TROPICAL SOUTH AMERICAN
  The name for this mahogany depends on the country in which it is harvested. If it came from Honduras, then it is Honduran mahogany; if Brazil, then it is Brazilian mahogany, etc.
  Source: South America
  Color: Light red or yellow-brown to a rich dark red
  Pattern: Mostly straight grain, some figures.

MAPLE. Also NORTHERN, ROCK, SUGAR, or BLACK
  Source: United States and Canada
  Color: Cream to light red-brown
  Pattern: Usually straight grained, but available as birdseye, curly, and fiddleback

MYRTLE, ACACIA, BAYTREE, CALIFORNIA LAUREL, or PEPPERWOOD
- Source: United States
- Color: Golden-brown and yellow-green
- Pattern: Mostly sold as burl

NARRA, AMBOYNA, ANGSENA, or SENA
- Source: East Indies and Philippines
- Color: Rose to deep red, golden yellow
- Pattern: Distinct grain, some ripple, burls

OAK, RED
- Source: United States
- Color: Slightly red tinge
- Pattern: Flaky figure

OAK, WHITE
- Source: United States
- Color: Light brown with gray tinge
- Pattern: Closer grained than red oak; occasional crotches, swirls, and burls

OAK, ENGLISH BROW . Also EUROPEAN or POLLARD
- Source: England
- Color: Light tan to deep brown
- Pattern: Noticeable figure and grain

ORIENTALWOOD. Also AUSTRALIAN LAUREL or WALNUT
- Source: Australia
- Color: Pink-grey to brown
- Pattern: Plain to highly figured with dark stripes

PADOUK or VERMILLION
- Source: Burma
- Color: Yellow and gold-red with brown
- Pattern: Interlocked grain producing cross figure on quartered section

PALDOA or DAO
- Source: Philippines
- Color: Gray to red-brown
- Pattern: Irregular stripes, occasional crotch or swirl

PEARWOOD
- Source: United States and Europe
- Color: Rosy cream; distinct leafy grain
- Pattern: Sometimes mottled

PECAN
- Source: United States
- Color: Red-brown
- Pattern: Distinct grain

PEROBA RED or PALO ROSA
- Source: Brazil
- Color: Pale rose with dark streaks
- Pattern: Dark streaks

PERSIMMON
- Source: United States
- Color: Light brown with darker stripes
- Pattern: Distinct grain

PINE, WHITE
- Source: United States
- Color: Cream to light red-brown
- Pattern: Straight and knotty grain

PRIMAVERA, DURANGO, PALO BLANCA, SAN JUAN, or WHITE MAHOGANY
- Source: Central America
- Color: Yellow-white to yellow-brown
- Pattern: Straight grain

REDWOOD
- Source: United States
- Color: Pink to deep red
- Pattern: Clusters of burls

ROSEWOOD, BRAZILIAN. Also RIO and BAHIA or JACARANDA
- Source: Brazil
- Color: Various shades of dark brown — chocolate to violet
- Pattern: Streaks of dark brown or black pigment lines

ROSEWOOD, EAST INDIAN , BOMBAY, BLACKWOOD, or MALOBAR
- Source: Southern India and Ceylon
- Color: Dark purple to ebony
- Pattern: Streaks of red or yellow

18

ROSEWOOD, HONDURAS
    Source: Central America
    Color: Lighter than Brazilian
    Pattern: Pink-brown or purple; streaked with darker and lighter bands

SAPELE, ABOUDIKRO, SIPO, or TIAMA
    Source: Africa
    Color: Dark red-brown
    Pattern: Stripe and bee's wing

SATINWOOD
    Source: Ceylon
    Color: Pale gold
    Pattern: Straight stripe, bee's wing mottled

TEAK. Also BURMA, GENUINE, or RANGOON
    Source: India
    Color: Tawny yellow to dark brown, often with lighter streaks
    Pattern: Sometimes mottled and fiddleback

TULIPWOOD, BOISE DE ROSE, PINKWOOD, or PALO ROSA
    Source: Brazil
    Color: Light background
    Pattern: Streaked with red and yellow

WALNUT, AMERICAN or BLACK
    Source: United States and Canada
    Color: Light grey-brown to dark purple-brown
    Pattern: Plain to highly figured

WALNUT, CLARO
    Source: United States
    Color: Tan-brown with dark brown
    Pattern: Wavy grain

WALNUT, FRENCH
    Source: France
    Color: Soft and quite gray-brown
    Pattern: Lighter in color than American walnut; fine smooth grain

WENGE, DIKELA, or PALLISSANDRE
    Source: Brazil
    Color: Dark brown with fine
    Pattern: Close, blackish veining

YEW, ENGLISH
    Source: England
    Color: Red-brown to rose red
    Pattern: Straight grain to wavy, burls and pips

ZEBRAWOOD, ZEBRANO, or ZINGANA
    Source: Africa
    Color: Straw and dark brown
    Pattern: Dark brown striped

NOTES

Veneers are sliced anywhere from $\frac{1}{40}$" to $\frac{1}{28}$" and sometimes $\frac{1}{32}$" thick. Needless to say, anything less than $\frac{1}{28}$" is going to be a problem when it comes to sanding. More than once, I have had to remove a piece because sanding went completely through it. In a later chapter, there is an explanation of how to remove and replace a damaged part.

Chemical reaction and dyes are used to change the colors of wood. As of a few years ago, there was only one company that could dye veneers with colors that were permanent. This company, located in Europe, will not reveal the process. The pigment in dyed veneers is dispersed evenly throughout the wood, causing a loss of character in grain and pattern. When restoring some antique objects, I noted that the dyed woods have faded. In some cases, the surface of the wood had reverted to its original color. Sanding through the surface provided an inkling of the original tint of each piece, and I was able to duplicate its original design.

Certain chemicals will react to the tannic acid naturally inherent in the wood. The shade of the veneer varies according to the chemical used, and the intensity of the color will depend on the acid contents in the veneer. For example, potassium dichromate will change mahogany to a dark red, and ammonia will change oak to a brownish gray. The advantage of chemically changing the color of the veneer is that the grain and characteristics of the wood will not be lost, and the natural beauty of the wood will remain. A complete list of all of the chemicals that it is possible to use to change the color of wood and the results is beyond the scope of this book.

ROSEWOOD can be a problem veneer because it contains natural oils that sometimes inhibit the gluing and finishing process. I have a picture on my wall with rosewood interspersed throughout the scene. These pieces should have been washed with gasoline or lacquer thinner to remove the oils, but this was neglected. All of these pieces have stayed in place but separated from the core piece of plywood. This separation can be detected by placing the project at a flat angle to a light source, such as a window, and noting the reflected light as pressure is applied to the piece. These oils also inhibit the drying qualities of the finish.

The sanding dust of some of the brightly colored veneers, such as PADOUK, has a tendency to run into the pores of adjacent veneers. Before sanding, it is wise to seal the grain of this and the adjacent lighter veneers with a sanding sealer. Remove this sanding dust from the pores with a soft brush and vacuum cleaner right after sanding.

GABOON EBONY and a few other veneers are scarce and sometimes hard to acquire. A careful check of the latest catalogs as soon as they arrive is sometimes rewarding, and rare items may be found.

4 • Making a Veneer Pad and Assembling the Veneers

Before any veneer can be cut, a pad consisting of the veneer leaf, a back-up board, and the sections of the pattern to be cut must be assembled. This pad permits the veneer to be cut without having it crack or chip.

My first few projects were kits that contained all of the materials to complete the picture. In these kits were some sheets of ⅛"-thick wood that was usually poplar. They served to back up and protect the veneer as it was being cut. The kits also contained a number of duplicates of the pattern; most of these were used as patterns for cutting the veneers, and the cut pieces of veneer were then cemented to one of the patterns.

In a process similar to that used for an original marquetry picture, each section of the design in these kit patterns was cut out of the copies with scissors at approximately ¼" beyond the saw-cutting line. Then these paper pieces were rubber cemented to the piece of poplar backing. The veneer was placed between this sheet of poplar with the cemented copy sections facing outward, and another sheet of poplar backing. This sandwich was fastened together with solid-brass 15-gauge escutcheon pins (round-headed nails). Holes were drilled slightly smaller than the diameter of the pins and spaced about a half-inch apart near to and outside of the cutting line. The holes were drilled so they would not split the veneer. After the pins were inserted, they were peened or rivetted over to hold the pad together, and so that they would not extend below the level of the backing and snag on the saw table top.

All coping saws can be adjusted to increase or decrease the saw blade tension. I usually cut the veneer with a light tension to minimize saw breakage. The blade then has a tendency to follow the grain in the backing wood, which adds to the difficulty in following the cutting line. I solved this problem by replacing the backing wood with illustration or poster board, which has

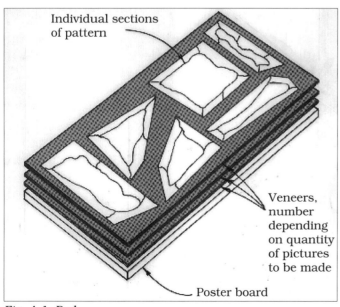

Fig. 4-1. Pad.

Individual sections of pattern

Veneers, number depending on quantity of pictures to be made

Poster board

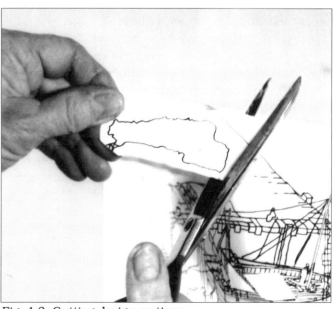

Fig. 4-2. Cutting design sections

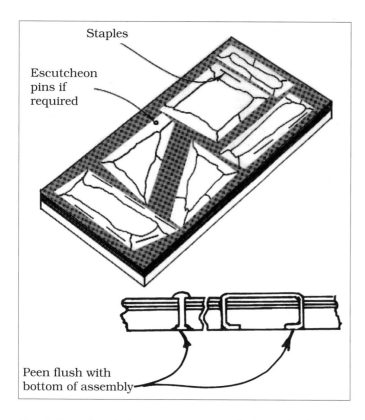

Fig. 4-3. Pad and pins, cross-section of pin or staple assembly

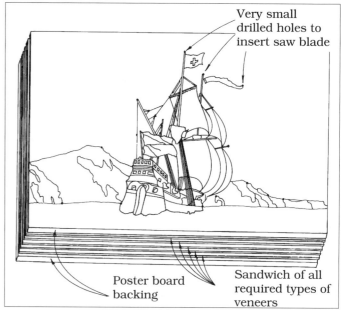

Fig. 4-4. Cutting, using a single pad.

no grain. There is no need for backing on the top of the veneer because the saw blade cuts on the downward stroke, so I rubber cement the pattern directly to the veneer. I replaced the pinning process with stapling by hand, which is much faster, although the staples still have to be hammered flat so that they do not snag on the saw table top. If, for some reason, the thickness of the assembly goes beyond the limits of the stapler, then the escutcheon pins must be used.

In summary, this assembly is called a pad, and consists of a veneer or veneers with the design section cemented to the top, a poster-board backing underneath, and all of the layers stapled together. Each individual can decide whether to complete all the cutting and then rubber cement the pieces to the reversed image copy, or cement separate pieces as the cutting proceeds.

Alternative Pad Assemblies

Another method of sawing cuts all of the veneers for a picture in a single-sawing operation. This technique requires a backing on

both top and bottom so that the veneer is not marred in the peening operation. All of the various veneers required in the picture are layered between the two backings. This pad will be thick and probably require escutcheon pins to hold it together. The holes for the pins will be obvious; so they must be located either on the cutting lines, or someplace in the picture where they will not be detrimental. The saw blade can cut through the soft brass pins without breaking.

A copy of the complete design is cemented to the top backing. After all of the cutting is complete, the result will be a box of picture components similar to jigsaw puzzle parts. Shapes will be duplicated, each one of a different veneer. Rubber cement one of each shape to the reversed copy of the design. Be careful to place contrasting veneers next to each other; avoid putting pieces of the same wood next to each other unless there is a good reason to do so. It is possible to make a number of pictures, all of the same pattern but each having a different wood in each section of the picture.

The method used by the commercial manu-facturers consists of layering the veneers with the grain in all of them running in the same direction. One leaf of veneer is required for each picture. Marquetry producers in Sorrento, Italy, cut pads with up to twenty-four slices of veneer in one pad assembly. After trying all cutting tech-

22

niques, I prefer this method, although I usually limit myself to doing one picture at a time. Today's furniture companies use this technique with a computer-controlled laser beam to cut the veneers.

For this method, the combination of backing and veneer is pinned or stapled together. The individual pieces of the design are cut out of the paper pattern copies and separated according to the kind of wood from which each will be cut. These paper pieces are rubber cemented to the top of the appropriate veneer; obviously, the grain of the wood must run in the direction that is wanted in the final picture. The direction of the wood grain needs to be checked again when pinning the veneers together. A pad must be made for each type of veneer that will be used in the picture. Again, it is best to pick out the veneer for the largest area of the design and make a pad for it first, and then make additional pads for increasingly smaller areas.

Cutting out the Veneers

Some craftsmen do all of their cutting with a utility craft knife and blades. My own experience cutting veneers with such a knife was not very successful; I had problems with the harder woods cracking and chipping. Now, I only use a knife for straight lines and a coping saw for everything else.

Bevel cutting the veneers results in a very close match of adjacent parts. Neighboring pieces of veneer are overlapped, cemented together with airplane glue, and cut simultaneously. The cut is made at an angle of about 10 degrees, depending on the thickness of the veneer and the blade. My experience with this method has convinced me that the only way to get the correct angle is by trial and error, taking into account the thickness of the saw blade and the thickness of the veneer. After cutting, the two veneers can be separated with a thin-bladed knife, and the parts are then cemented to a reversed copy of the picture.

As mentioned previously, do not make the saw blade too taut; less tension will minimize blade breakage. Also do not apply too much force when pushing the saw pad into the blade; LET THE SAW TEETH DO THE CUTTING. If the blade

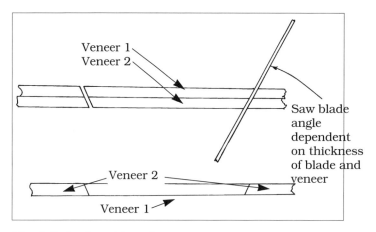

Fig. 4-5. Angle cutting of components.

has to be forced through the pad in order to cut it, the blade is probably dull.

Each craftsman can decide what to do with the design parts as they are cut. I sometimes cut all the parts and place each kind of veneer in a plastic dish. I will then assemble each picture on the reversed copy after I am completely through with the cutting. Other times — just to vary the routine — I will cement each piece to the reverse copy as I cut. No matter how it is done, the largest pieces, usually sky or sea, should be cemented to the reversed copy first. They govern where the smaller sections will go as they are cemented to the reversed copy.

If the cutting has been done carefully, all of the various pieces of veneer should fit together nicely and provide a complete mirror image of the picture; its right side is facing the mirror-image copy of the picture. If some of the parts do not fit together tidily, it is possible to trim them with sandpaper at the interfering edges. Gaps can be

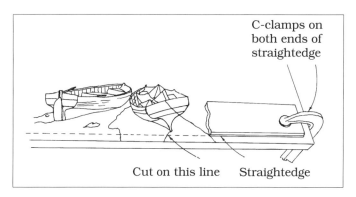

Fig. 4-6. Trimming edge of picture.

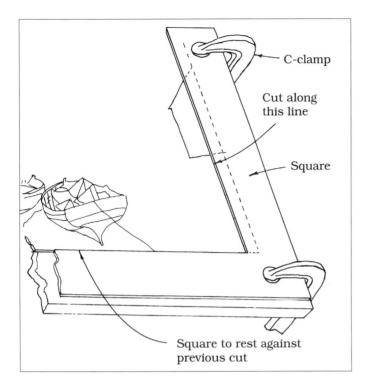

C-clamp

Cut along
this line

Square

Square to rest against
previous cut

Fig. 4-7. Cutting Corners with a square.

filled with a paste mixture of glue and sanding dust of one of the adjacent woods. There will be a second chance to fill these gaps after the veneers are glued to the plywood core and the sanding process has begun.

Getting the Edges Even

After all of the pieces of the picture have been glued to the reversed copy, the outermost edges of the picture will be somewhat ragged. The picture must be trimmed perfectly square and to the correct size; otherwise, the corner miters will not meet at the corners of both picture and border. Remember that when the pattern was inked onto the vellum, instructions said to make the outside edges ¼-inch larger. Now that ¼-inch can be trimmed off to make perfectly straight edges and 90-degree angles on the corners.

Using a metal straight edge, cut through the picture along the top using a utility knife or scalpel. The knife will be cutting through soft and hard woods in this operation, which is harder to control than cutting through one or the other. Do not force the cut; it is better to make many passes with the blade over the veneer rather than one or two. If the blade breaks, it means too much pressure is being applied.

Using that edge as a base for the combination square, cut the two sides adjoining that original side to right angles and the correct size. Finally, mark the vertical dimensions of the picture at each end along each of the two new cuts. Connect those two marks with the straight edge, and trim off the bottom. I like to place the straight edge or combination square on top of the veneer, and clamp them to the top of the workbench with "C" clamps. This technique prevents any chance of the picture's slipping, and as many passes as necessary can be made to complete the cut.

When this process is complete, the veneer and paper backing will be cut through completely, the edges of the picture will be perfectly even, and the corners will be exactly 90 degrees.

5 • Choosing and Making the Borders

There are many border arrangements, and four of the most common appear in the following drawings. Fig. 5-1A illustrates the usual way with four veneers of equal width, the grain running parallel to the sides of the picture and the corners mitered. Fig. 5-1B has equal width borders with the grains at right angles to the edge of the picture. Fig. 5-1C has all the grain running parallel to the sides of the picture and requires mitering a large single leaf of veneer. Fig. 5-1D has the grain diagonal across the corners and meeting at the center of the borders, no mitering; but close fitting is required where borders come together.

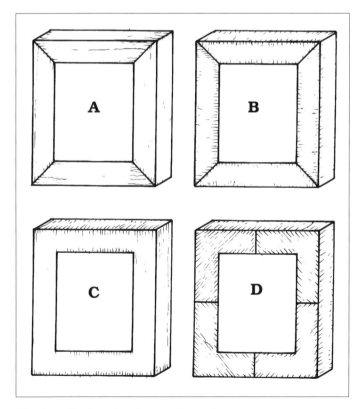

Fig. 5-1. Various border configurations.

Marquetry uses a very thin border called a *stringer*, which is a narrow ⅛" to ¼" strip of contrasting veneer, and a wider *border* that functions like a picture frame to edge pictures after the veneers have been assembled. The choice is up to the craftsman; he can dispense with either one if he desires. If a border is used, it should not be made of fancy or highly figured veneers as they draw attention away from the picture. The eye must be attracted to the subject of the scene first and foremost. The wood for the borders should be straight grained, and the kind of wood used should depend on the color the craftsman wants to use: oak or sycamore for a light border, walnut or sapele for a medium shade, and gaboon ebony or wenge for a dark border.

Workmanship is also very important. Nothing will attract the eye quicker than an obvious error or bad technique in the border. Sloppy corner joints will stick out like a sore thumb. I can sometimes ignore an error in the picture, but a similar error in the border will get my attention and action. I have redone more borders than any other parts of projects.

I usually put a stringer between the border and the picture. It provides an added touch and delineates the two areas of the project. Most veneer houses sell ready-made stringers, but most of these are quite elaborate and draw attention away from the picture.

Making the Stringer and Border

The same technique is used in making both the stringer and the border. To cut a straight line on one edge of the veneer for the stringer, clamp the straightedge and veneer to the cutting board with "C" clamps. These clamps prevent any

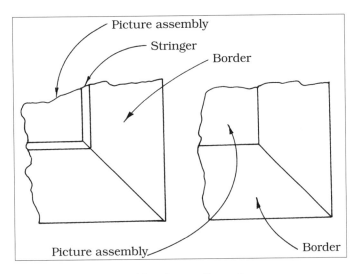

Fig. 5-2. Stringer and border configurations.

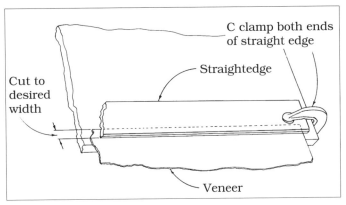

Fig. 5-3. Method of cutting miter or border.

movement during the cutting operation. Slice the opposite edge by moving the straightedge the width of the stringer, clamp it down again, and cut. The length must be an inch or two longer than the edge of the picture where it will be placed to allow for its mitering and trimming. The wide border strip is handled the same way, but its length is extended farther to compensate for the larger miter. The width of the border is up to the craftsman and may differ with each picture. I usually use a narrow edge (about ¾") because I think it accents the picture very well. It does, however, need to be cut about a half-inch wider than the width wanted for the finished project in order to allow the border to be trimmed after the veneer is glued to the backing.

Attaching the Stringer and Border

To attach the stringer and border to the veneer assembly, put a strip of 1-inch-wide masking tape along the back edge of the picture for its full length. Make sure the tape is wide enough to attach both the stringer and the border to it. Lay the stringer and border against one edge of the picture, and press them into the tape. Make sure there is no gap between the picture, stringer, and border. The ends of these pieces must extend past the corners of the picture to allow for mitering and trimming.

If a stringer is not used, attach the border directly to the picture.

Follow the same procedure on one of the adjacent sides, allowing the stringer and border

strips of the two sides to overlap. To miter the corners, first note the point of the 90-degree angle of the corner of the picture and the place where the outermost edges of the border pieces come together. Set the straightedge on these two locus points, and clamp it and the veneer to the cutting board. To minimize gaps in the seam, keep the scalpel vertical and cut along the straightedge. This will make a 45-degree cut. Do not force the cut; make many passes. Turn the picture and secure the miter together with masking tape. Follow the same procedure on all four edges and corners of the picture.

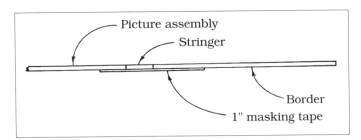

Fig. 5-4. A method of attaching the picture, stringer, and border.

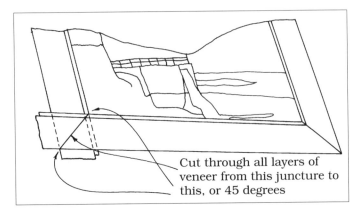

Fig. 5-5. Mitering procedure.

If these instructions have been followed carefully, all of the paper, tape, etc. that are part of the assembly will be on the back of the picture. The face or glue side (the reverse of the finished picture) will be clean and clear of anything that will affect the gluing phase.

Filling in Gaps

If there are any gaps where veneers come together, they can be filled with sanding dust and glue at this time. The dust is made by rubbing a piece of scrap veneer on a sheet of 100-grit sandpaper. The veneers on either side of the gap dictate which veneer to use for the dust: if a subdued or hidden juncture is required, use the same kind of wood as the veneer adjoining the gap. If, for some reason, the seam needs to be highlighted, use a veneer with a contrasting color. This dust is mixed with aliphatic resin glue. The consistency should be like putty so that the color of the wood dominates. A thin mixture is easier to use, but the color of the glue will be too visible. Be sure this glued part of the picture's surface is smooth and has no projections after the glue is dry. Some light sanding may be required to even the surface. There is one more chance to fill gaps after the picture comes out of the veneer press and the finishing stage begins.

The combination assembly of picture and border is now complete and the picture is ready for the gluing process.

6 • Gluing and Finishing

The veneer assembly now needs to be glued to a cabinet-grade ⅜" piece of plywood known as the core. This piece will be the middle of a sandwich of veneers and should be about ¼" to ½" larger than the picture itself so that the core can be trimmed.

The same type of gluing operations are performed on both sides of the core at the same time to prevent warping. In other words, when the veneer assembly of picture and border is ready to glue to the top surface of the core, a piece of veneer that is larger than the core must be glued to the bottom surface of the core. The backing veneer can be anything extra that is in stock. If the width of the picture requires more than one leaf for this backing, the mating edges of two leaves can butt together or overlap, and will not be noticeable after subsequent sanding. Use a strip of masking tape on the side that will not be glued in order to hold two leaves of veneer together.

Cementing this extra veneer to the back of the core serves to counteract the stresses caused by the gluing operation on the face of the picture, thereby reducing the chance of the picture's warping sometime in the future.

For a satisfactory gluing job, two gluing pads are needed to distribute the clamping pressure evenly over the surface of the veneers. Each of these pads is made of approximately 75 newspaper sheets cut a little larger than the dimensions of the picture assembly. The final sheet that will be next to the veneer should be of waxed paper. There should be no creases, folds, or half sheets among the newspapers; any fold in the paper may cause an uneven surface and require extra sanding for a smooth face. The waxed paper prevents the pads from being glued to the veneers and the wood from being discolored by the newsprint. One of these pads is placed between the caul of the press, and the picture and border assembly. The other is used on the bottom with the waxed paper next to the back of the picture.

The Gluing Process

To glue the project together, first place the cross pieces of the veneer press underneath the lower caul. As a reminder, a newspaper pad with a piece of waxed paper is facing up and positioned near the center of the caul. The backing veneer is centered on top of the waxed paper of the pad with the side to be glued facing up. Now, use the toothed glue spreader to distribute a thin layer of aliphatic resin glue evenly over the entire area of one side of the plywood core. Place this side down on top of the backing veneer. Be sure that the veneer extends past the edges of the plywood on all four sides.

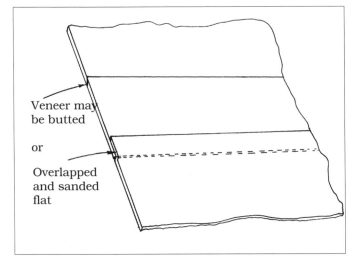

Veneer may be butted

or

Overlapped and sanded flat

Fig. 6-1. A drawing of the veneer of the back of a project.

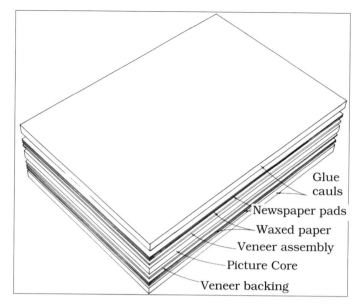

Fig. 6-2. Arrangement of components of project, and necessary pads for gluing.

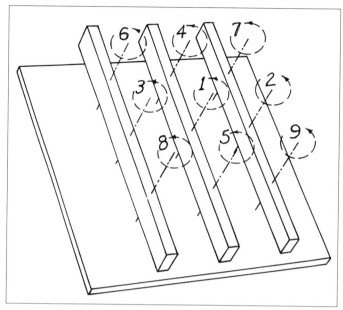

Fig. 6-4. Press screws tightening sequence.

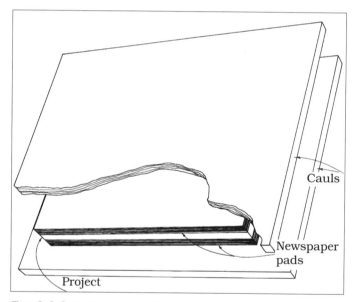

Fig. 6-3.Components in glue press.

Then apply a coating of the same glue to the top of the plywood, and lay the picture and border combination on that with the side to be glued facing down, of course. Be sure that the core extends past the veneer on four sides. On top of all this, position a layer of waxed paper, a newspaper pad, and the top caul of the press.

The method of applying pressure in clamping depends on what kind of press is used. The press with the bowed cross pieces requires that the "C" clamps at the center be tightened first and then

that pressure is gradually worked out to the end of the press. The clamps need to be tightened until the arc of the bow in the cross piece is flattened and pressure is being applied to the edge of the cauls.

The press using the "Pony" press screws requires a slightly different approach. The screws at the center must be tightened first and, again, worked out to the outer edges of the press. The purpose, in both cases, is to force any excess glue or air bubbles to move to the outer edges.

Trimming the Edges

Allow 24 hours for the glue to dry before taking the project out of the press. The picture must now be trimmed to the proper dimensions. This operation should be performed on a table saw so that a perfectly straight and smooth line is present on all four sides. If a saw is not available, a woodworking shop will do it for a fee.

First, decide what the final width of the border will be. Measure out that distance all around the picture and draw a line on all four sides. Outside of this line on the bottom border, draw another parallel line about ⅛" to ¼" below. Using a scroll saw with a heavy blade, carefully cut along the outside bottom parallel line. This edge will furnish a starting point for trimming the picture.

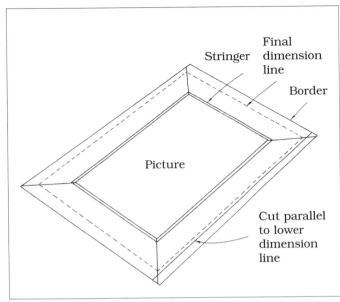

Fig. 6-5. Trimming the project.

Set this sawed edge against the rip fence of the table saw and adjust the fence so that the table saw will cut along the dimension line on the top of the picture. After making this cut, put the top edge against the rip fence and adjust the fence to cut along the dimension line on the bottom of the picture. This will remove the original ⅛" to ¼" used as a starting line. The ends can now be trimmed by setting either the top or bottom against a 90-degree miter gauge on the table saw and cutting to the dimension lines.

The edges of the border, core, and backing will all be even at this point.

Covering the Edges

The exposed ends of the plywood core need to be covered for a professional result. This operation requires two 1" x 1" glue cauls that are about an inch longer than the longest edge of the picture. Two bar clamps are also needed. Cut four strips of the same veneer that was used in the border (or a veneer that will contrast with the border) about ⅛" wider than the thickness of the core and veneer assembly. Two strips need to be slightly longer than the width of the assembly, and two need to be longer than the length. These pieces are glued to the outside edges of the assembly with bar clamps, gluing opposite edges at the same time. The gluing area is small enough that newspaper pads are not necessary, but waxed paper is needed between the veneer and the 1" x 1" cauls.

After the glue on the edges has dried overnight, the edges and ends of the strips need to be sanded down so that they are flush with the adjoining surfaces of the picture. The edges do not have to be trimmed at this time, but smoothing them will prevent their being chipped in subsequent operations. Go through the same procedure for all four sides of the picture. Sand all edges flush with adjoining surfaces. Sharp corners have a tendency to chip or crack, so they should be rounded with sandpaper. Take great care not to break through the veneer.

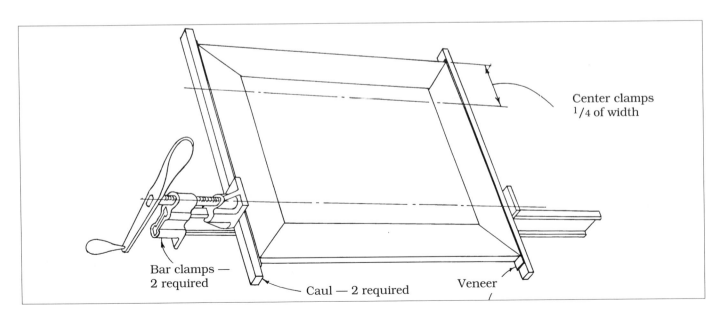

Fig. 6-6. The technique of edge gluing.

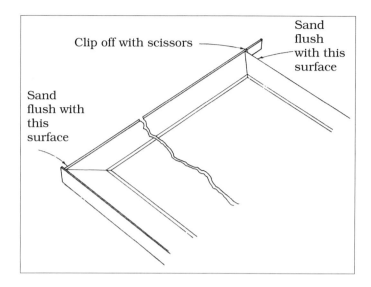

Fig. 6-7. Trimming the edges.

Finishing and Preserving the Surfaces

Wood finishing is a rather personal process; everyone seems to have his or her favorite method. The following process is the one I developed after much experimentation.

Do preliminary sanding with 120- or 100-grit paper. The veneer on the back is meant to provide a pleasing-looking cover over the plywood core and is not as important as the front. If veneer leaves on the back have been overlapped, they should be sanded smooth. Follow the grain of the wood as much as possible when sanding; cross-grain sanding will leave minute scratches that are not easy to eliminate. This primary sanding is all that is necessary for the back of the picture.

The face and edges of the picture will be viewed by friends and neighbors, so they require much more care in finishing. The first thing to do is to remove the pattern cemented to the front surface of the picture. It is possible to dislodge the paper in the sanding procedure, but it is less time consuming if the paper is stripped off. This process can be made easier by soaking the paper with rubber cement thinner. Masking tape should not be removed from the surface unless it has been saturated with thinner, otherwise the tape's adhesive will pick up the soft portion of the wood grain and pull it out of the wood.

The preliminary sanding is done with 120- or 100-grit paper, but it will be difficult always to sand with the grain except for the borders because the inside sections of the picture will have grain that runs in random directions. A good example is the left and right borders. These edges have to be sanded horizontally with the grain of the border. Obviously, this causes some cross-grain sanding inside the edge of the picture. The only way to get around this problem is to limit the primary sanding. Do most of the work with a finer-grade abrasive paper such as a 150- or 200-grit.

After completing this sanding phase, any gaping joints not filled must be filled now with a mixture of sanding dust and glue as noted in Chapter 5. Any roughness created by the filling process will have to be sanded away.

Use a polyurethane finishing product that is as clear as possible when the can is opened in order to preserve the beautiful original colors of the veneers. Since all these finishes have an amber tone to them, choose one with the least obvious color and it will not noticeably affect the color of the veneer. There is a colorless water-based polyurethane finish available, but it leaves a slight milky cast after drying.

One or two coats of finish are sufficient for the back and edges of the picture. After the first application of finish is dry, it might enhance the picture to add some contrasting lines to it — for example, cordage or rigging on a sailing ship, cables on a suspension bridge, etc. This is done by cutting the lines of the rigging into the wood with a scalpel and accenting these cuts with a sharp pencil lead, or filling them in with glue and sawdust of a contrasting color. If the lines are to be subtle, the slight contrast provided by the finish itself as it fills in the cut will suffice. Do not try to use a stain or powdered pencil lead because it tends to get into the pores of the wood and does not provide a sharp line. The finish that was previously applied helps to confine the line to the cut area. Another layer of finish is now applied and allowed to dry.

The balance of the finishing will be accomplished by lightly spraying the picture with water and rubbing it with 400-grit wet or dry sandpaper. The water serves as a lubricant in the finishing operation and also alleviates the tendency of the abrasive paper to clog up.

After sanding, another coat of polyurethane is applied, and the sanding process repeated. This cycle is continued until the surface is perfectly smooth. I usually run this sequence about a dozen times before I am satisfied. The finish will have filled all uneven areas in the picture, and no imperfections should be seen when the picture is viewed from an acute angle.

As a final step, I like to cut the glare of the finish by rubbing it with automotive polishing compound, or applying a final coat of satin-finish polyurethane.

7 • Restoring and Repairing Marquetry

The ability to restore or repair existing pieces of marquetry or any wood surface is a useful skill to develop. However, this type of work can require tools other than those needed for making marquetry pictures. Sometimes inlay skills might be needed for certain types of restoration or repair. Several of my favorite repair and restoration projects are described in this chapter.

Repairing an Oak Table

My latest repair project was a damaged table that I purchased for a very reasonable price. The distressed top had two deep gouges that went through the surface of oak veneer and into the core wood. Using a paste of sawdust and glue, I completely filled in the deep holes until they were level with the top of the veneer. After drying for 24 hours, the filled area was routed with a hand motor tool and router attachment using a ⅛"

straight bit. In this kind of repair, the area that is to have matching veneer inlaid needs to be routered to a depth of a little less than the thickness of the veneer. A piece of oak in my veneer inventory closely matched the grain and color of the table top.

A pattern for each of the two repair areas was made by covering the recesses with tracing paper and drawing along the edges with a blunted pencil lead (Figure 7-1). A carpenter's pencil with the lead sanded flat makes a good marking tool for this process.

The patterns were then rubber cemented to an area of oak veneer that closely matched the grain and markings of the wood on the table top. It is important that rubber cement not get on the face of the pattern as it will remove the pencil lines. I stapled the pattern and veneer to a poster board backing and cut along the line on the pattern with a coping saw. The veneer did require some final fitting into the recesses, which was done by sanding the edges where interference occurred. When veneers are cut for this kind of repair, it is always better to make them a little too big than too small.

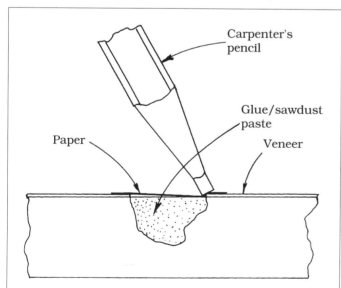

Fig. 7-1. Outlining the routered area.

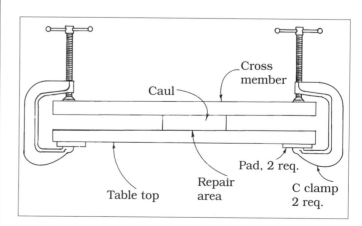

Fig. 7-2. A technique for applying localized pressure.

Gluing pressure was applied according to the illustration in Figure 7-5. After sanding the repairs smooth, two coats of finish were applied over the whole table top. The repair was hardly noticeable; the table was now functional and did not need the extensive finishing process that I normally use in marquetry projects.

Repairing Blisters

Occasionally, for some reason, veneer will separate from its wooden core and develop blisters. These areas may be repaired by slitting the blister along the grain with a thin knife or razor blade. Use a glue injector (available from a marquetry supplies company) to work glue through the slit and into the blistered zone. Clamping or weighting down the gluing pad may require some ingenuity to provide the needed pressure. Some helpful items might be "C" clamps or even a pail of water. I know of a case where one wheel of a car was parked on the gluing caul, but this would only work on a flat piece. No matter how it is done, waxed paper between the pressure pad and the veneer is required. Sanding with fine sandpaper and standard refinishing procedures will provide an invisible repair.

Slitting the blister provides some idea of the thickness of the veneer, and the amount of sanding should be judged accordingly. Sanding through the veneer will require a more extensive repair.

Restoring Antique Barrel Organs

I have had the pleasure of restoring four antique barrel organs, commonly called "monkey" or "street" organs. In past centuries, these instruments were carried through city streets, quite often with a monkey perched on top. The monkey would pass around either a tin cup or his hat after the concert, hence the name "monkey" organ. The man who provided the music was known as an "organ grinder," possibly because he looked as though he were grinding coffee as he turned the handle of the organ. At the risk of dating myself, I can remember seeing and hearing these performances (and donating to the monkey) on the streets of Brooklyn.

Fig. 7-3. Organ, Monkey, and Organ grinder.

How the machine moved through the streets depended on its size. The smaller one was carried with the aid of a shoulder strap and rested on a single collapsible leg as it was being played. The larger machine was too heavy to carry and was wheeled around on a small cart.

Because of the environment and rough use to which these machines were subjected, the cabinets had to be constructed ruggedly. The corners were dovetailed, glued, and protected with ornamental brass escutcheon plates. The fact that most organs were rented did not improve the care that the instruments received. Of the four that I have rebuilt, only one was in such a condition that the original cabinet could be used.

Frati Barrel Organ

My first project was a Frati built in Berlin in the 1880's. This machine, minus its mechanical parts, was given to me for repair in a box. The case was in small pieces, but there were enough of them so that overall dimensions could be determined. Rebuilding the cabinet itself was done by another person so all I had to contend

Fig. 7-4. A Frati barrel organ.

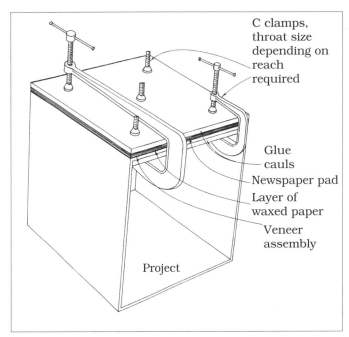

Fig. 7-5. A clamping arrangement.

with was the marquetry. I was able to ascertain most of the marquetry design from the parts in the box. The balance of the layout was determined from a copy of the original sales brochure of the machine. The kinds of veneers used were detected by sanding some of the pieces, and then comparing the grain and color with photographs in *Fine Hardwoods Selectorama*. This cabinet made extensive use of rosewood veneer — with its inherent gluing and finishing problems.

Gluing the assembled veneer design to the case required extra care. It was possible to glue only one side at a time, and it was imperative that the veneer stay in its place as the glue cauls and clamps were applied. I spread the glue on the side of the cabinet and secured the veneer assembly in place with masking tape. No veneer or finish was required on the inside of the cabinet as its construction precluded any warpage. However, a close-fitting caul was required on the inside of the cabinet to distribute the gluing pressure evenly and provide a complete back-up over the whole gluing area. A wax paper layer, newspaper pad, and caul were required on the outside of the veneer. The pressure was applied by deep-throated "C" clamps for the centers and smaller ones for the edges. After the gluing process was complete, I filled the gaps between veneers with a matching sawdust and glue paste.

The woodworking phase of the project was completed with the cycles of sanding and coats of finish as described in Chapter 6.

Some of the brass work, such as escutcheon plates, etc., had to be replaced. I bought flat brass of the correct thickness at a local hobby store and cut out the shapes with a coping saw, using a standard metal-cutting blade. Before replacing the brass work, I gave it a high polish with a cloth wheel and rouge, and then spray-coated it with clear plastic.

Molinari Barrel Organ (1)

Another case that I rebuilt was a smaller Molinari built in Brooklyn, New York, in about 1900. This case had been scorched in a fire, and there were some cracks on one end; otherwise, it was in fair condition. By sanding off the charred and aged surface of the veneer, I was able to determine the configuration of the design and the types of woods used. I then removed all of the old veneer by applying a hot iron to it to soften the glue and then peeling the veneer off. Wide cracks at the end of the cabinet were filled in with glue, but they came back to haunt me later.

The front of this machine had a design of flowers and foliage, but the sides and back were

Fig. 7-6. The Molinari barrel organ (1).

simply covered with plain mahogany. When these sections were restored, the case was ready for sanding and finishing; but the veneer covering the old cracks split again in exactly the same place where the original fractures had occurred. I removed the veneer and cleaned out the glue in

Fig. 7-7. The Jul. Hein. Zimmerman barrel organ.

the cracks. Then, I enlarged the splits and glued a thin strip of wood into each of them. This strip was the same width as the thickness of the case wall. I am not sure why the original repair did not hold up, but there was a heavy concentration of glue in the cracks. I surmise it was because of the different expansion rates of the glue and wood.

Most of the brass work was missing on this machine, so I spent a lot of time replacing it.

Jul. Hein. Zimmerman Barrel Organ

My third project was a Jul. Hein. Zimmerman, built or distributed in Leipzig, Germany, during the 1800's. This machine had been partially destroyed; but again, there was enough of it left so that the dimensions of the cabinet and its marquetry design could be determined. I rebuilt this machine — cabinet and marquetry — completely. The original dimensions were determined from the old machine, and I could see that the cabinet was made of gumwood. I copied the construction of the original, using the same kind of wood, hand-making the dovetail joints to the same dimensions, etc.

The overall appearance of the veneer on the original was drab and had no color — bleached by sun and age. It was apparent that the veneer wood was of all the same type. However, sanding removed the faded surface of the veneer and revealed the original tints. I discovered that the case builder had used dyed veneers exclusively. I do not use dyed wood in making my own pictures, but a restoration project means that the item will be re-made as close to the original all respects as possible. Therefore, in this case, I used dyed woods that matched the originals. Modern dyed veneers are far less likely to fade than their counterparts from previous generations.

Molinari Barrel Organ (2)

The fourth machine was another Molinari. The veneer design was a geometric pattern and a parquetry, rather than marquetry, project. The configuration duplicated figures over the surface. Some of the elements of these shapes were minute and impossible to handle in my usual way. Fortunately, all of these tiny pieces were either rectangular or square. I cut strips of dyed veneer that were ⅟₃₂", ⅟₁₆", and ⅛" wide, all about six inches long. Then I glued these strips together along their edges so that the required design appeared at the ends. I sliced thin pieces off the end and cemented them to a master copy just as I do a cut piece of veneer for a marquetry project.

Some of the figures on this case were curved, and above and below the tier of strips were three layers of variously colored veneers. I cut six pieces of veneer of the required colors that were each 2 inches wide and 6 inches long. I dampened one side of each piece by placing a wet cloth on them; this caused them to curl. I dried these pieces in such a way that they held to the curve. Then I constructed a gluing press that confined the layers of veneer to the inside radius that was needed. Finally, the veneer segments plus the layer of thin strips — all of them coated with glue — were assembled and placed in the press.

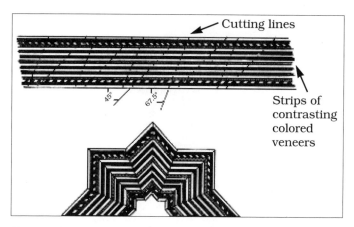

Fig. 7-10. A strip assembly.

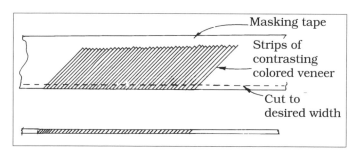

Fig. 7-8. An assembly of veneer strips.

Fig. 7-11. A special veneer press.

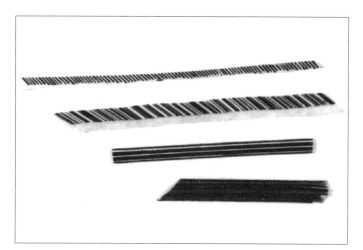

Fig. 7-9. A strip assembly.

Fig. 7-12. An assembly.

Fig. 7-13. Sliced segments from the curved assembly.

Fig. 7-14. Assembly of strip sections and curved segments.

Fig. 7-15. A second Molinari.

Modern tools and techniques provide many advantages over old methods used for parquetry and marquetry in past centuries. Restoring and repairing beautiful, hand-crafted antiques from the past is a very satisfying part of this hobby and a skill sought after by owners of lovely pieces of furniture and other items from the past.

8 • Glossary

Backing Base that the veneer is glued to, usually cabinet grade ⅜" plywood. Plain wood has a tendency to warp and should be avoided.

Birdsmouth Portable saw table to be used with a fret saw and frame.

Burl Severe distortion of grain usually resulting from overgrowth over dead branch stubs on the tree.

Caul Flat, cabinet grade plywood, at least as large as the veneer design; this caul is placed over the veneer to distribute the clamping pressure evenly over the whole area of the veneer when cementing to the core.

Crotch Distortion of grain at the juncture of two limbs of a tree.

Curly grain Fibers are distorted so as to appear curled, as in "birds eye maple."

Drawing Pen Pen for drawing on vellum. The "nib" dispenses the carbon black "india ink," ".018" indicates the diameter of the nib, and therefore the width of the line that it produces.

Escutcheon pin Round headed nail, usually of brass.

Flitch Leaves of veneer cut from one log and in the order that it was cut so that the color and grain is matched.

Fret saw Frame used to hold jewelers saw blades.

Grain Indicates the direction of the fibers of the wood. The grain can be straight, curly, spiral, mottled, swirled, fiddleback, peanut shell, crotch, burl, satiny, leafy, knotty, interlocking, rippled, figured, bee's wing, wavy, and pips.

Heartwood The inactive cells of a tree formed by the changes in the inner cells of the sapwood.

Inlay A design or pattern of wood veneer, shell, or any other material. The base wood of Mahogany, Rosewood, or some hard wood is routed and the design glued into the recess.

Leaf Sheet of veneer.

Locus Meeting point of two or more lines.

Marquetry A design or pattern of wood veneer, shell, or any other material, glued to and completely covering a surface.

Mat Layers of approximately 75 sheets of newspaper, for the purpose of evenly distributing gluing pressure over the surface of the veneer.

Miter Forty-five degree angle cut in mating strips of veneer to form ninety-degree corner.

Pad A pinned or stapled assembly of veneer leaf, back-up board, and the pieces of the design that indicate how the veneer is to be cut.

Pantograph An instrument for for the mechanical copying of plans, diagrams, etc.,at a reduced or enlarged scale.

Parquetry Same as marquetry except in a geometric design.

Pattern Master drawing or design of project.

Peened Rivetted, to secure end of escutcheon pin.

Pigment A coloring matter or substance.

Plain sliced The log is cut in half lengthwise and then sliced parallel to the flat surface of the log, producing a flitch.

Quarter cut The log is quartered and then sliced from the center of the outside arc of the log to the juncture of the quartering cuts, producing a flitch.

Rotary cut The log is rotated in a veneer machine and the leaves are peeled off in continues sheets as wide as the length of the log.

Sapwood The living cells and the active part of the life process of a tree.

Spiral grain The fibers take a spiral course about the trunk of the tree.

Straight grain The fibers run parallel to the axis of the tree trunk

Stringer Narrow ⅛" to ½" strip of veneer used between picture and border.

Stylus Sharp pointed steel instrument for marking.

Vellum A translucent matte finish paper or mylar film for rendering in pen and ink, pencil, etc.

Veneer A thin layer of wood of uniform thickness produced by peeling, slicing, or sawing.

Wavy grain The fibers collectively form undulations, and have a wavy appearance.

9 • Index